Prayer Banks

Ancient Secrets on how to make Prayer Deposits and Withdrawals!

By Uebert Snr Angel PhD

SpiritLibrary PUBLICATIONS

Unless otherwise stated, all scripture quotations are taken from the King James Version of the Bible.

ISBN 978-0-955 8116-6-1

Copyright 2014 by Uebert Snr Angel

Published by *SpiritLibrary* **Publications**

Printed in the United Kingdom of Great Britain. All rights reserved under International Copyright Law. Contents and or cover may not be reproduced in whole or in part in any form without the express written consent of the publisher.

Contents

Chapter One:
Understanding Prayer Banks 5

Chapter Two:
Prayer Banking Systems 21

Chapter Three:
Prayer Bank Overdrafts 43

Chapter Four:
Prayer Bank Joint Accounts 65

Chapter Five:
Prayer Bank Guarantees 75

Chapter Six:
Prayer Bank Transfers 87

Chapter Seven:
When you have to see the Bank Manager 95

CHAPTER ONE

Understanding PRAYER BANKS

Dr Yongi Cho, founder of the largest church on earth with almost 1 000 000 (one million) congregants has been using this for years and miracles, signs and wonders have followed him. He told me that when his church, Yoido Full Gospel Church, had reached about 300,000 active members, a pastor from a church with just 3,000 came to see him. The pastor said to him,

"Dr. Cho, I need help in understanding something. Like yourself, I'm Korean and a pastor of a church. But you have 300,000 members and I have 3,000, so something does not add up for me."

Then this pastor, without any hint of arrogance, began to compare his background with that of Dr. Cho.

"I have an American Education, you have studied only at a bible school here in Korea. In addition, I have examined, as objectively as I can, tape recordings of my sermons and of your sermons. I believe I preach a better sermon. What I don't understand is why, if I preach a better sermon and have a better education, do you have 300,000 members in your church and I have just 3,000 members?"

Dr Cho said that he answered with a question that began to unveil truth on the existence of prayer banks and how they can be used to move heaven and earth.

Dr. Cho asked;

"Do you Pray?"

"Oh, yes," the pastor said.

"How much do you pray?"

The pastor with no hesitation answered,

"I pray daily at least thirty minutes. I have outlined my prayers so that in the course of the week I will have prayed for all my obligations here and across the world. I am very, very conscientious about that."

After displaying the thirty minutes he spent in prayer on a daily basis, he noticed Dr. Cho's face was just as shining as ever so he decided to ask him a question.

"Now you know I pray thirty minutes but how much do you pray Dr. Cho?"

Dr. Cho answered.

"I pray between one hour to three hours a day"

Then Dr. Cho went on to drop the clincher. "The difference"

"The DIFFERENCE between THIRTY MINUTES in PRAYER and THREE HOURS in PRAYER is the DIFFERENCE BETWEEN 3,000 members and 300,000 members"

Dr Cho was now exposing that there was a need to deposit prayer if any person or any believer is to purchase anything from the heavens. It is a clear sign that when it comes to miracles in one's life, there needs to be adequate prayer that would have gone up for a miracle to be experienced here on earth. Prayer then is the currency of the kingdom of heaven and without a real prayer life your deposits in heaven are very little so when you face problems there will be no currency in your prayer bank account to cover for the miracle you need.

Prayer Banks

Just as we have deposits and withdrawals and also overdrafts in the earthly banks, the kingdom of God also seems to function that way when it comes to answered prayer. The less a believer prays, the more he becomes weak in the things of God and the things of life. The more a man prays, the bigger his deposits are in the spiritual realm.

This secret of prayer banks is a lantern on the stern for a lot of believers who want their prayer life to yield results. Whether you want a miracle or want to perform one, you should be aware of the ancient secrets of PRAYER BANKS that move heaven and earth.

This revelation has been used from way back even in the times of Elijah, Moses and even used by our Lord Jesus Christ Himself with miracles following without fail.

Accumulating Credit In The Spiritual Realm

When the Lord told me that I could accumulate credit in the spiritual banks through prayer it was mind blowing and very difficult for me to show the believers this secret. I was plain afraid of the persecution that comes with claiming exclusivity on something this big so when Dr Cho said it, I realised there were some men of God of great repute who knew about PRAYER BANKS. They might not call this revelation PRAYER BANKS but they sure understand the importance of depositing prayer.

You see the amount of prayer going to God is proportionate to the level of miracle you receive. A weak prayer life is answered by a weak miracle and a weak miracle is always a result of a weak prayer life!

The Day The Lord Taught Me On PRAYER BANKS

Beginning of 2008 in Ashton Under Lyne, United Kingdom was the place I had prayed to the Lord about how I wanted him to use me and to do miracles in my life. I prayed that the Lord would use me mightily in miracles that the world had never seen so that I could prove his existence to those who do not believe in his existence. It was something I felt in me that the Lord could be proven through his works more than just talk.

I remember how the whole room changed and I was taken into glory, beyond the curtain of time. I saw the streets of heaven, the beauty which no language on earth can describe. Even those with the highest academic degrees of linguistic abilities will fail. In fact I can definitely assure you that there is no language here on earth to describe such beauty. It would be a crime to compare it to this carcus we call earth.

As I moved in the streets, the angelic being I had said he needed to take me to a certain place where I would see the saints. That brought joy to me. I have always been fascinated by the likes of Smith Wigglesworth, Kenneth E. Hagin, Kathlyne Kulman, William Marrion Branham and Maria Woodworth Etter. These are saints who managed to never let the world control them. Only God controlled them and only God ruled their lives.

At the speed of the agreement that we are going to see the saints, we seemed like we moved at the speed of thought and there we were. I saw Smith Wigglesworth, Kenneth E. Hagin, Kathryne Kulman, William Marrion Branham and Maria Woodworth Etter in a park-like area with modern artifacts, but at the same time looked antique but here I mean really beautiful and posh antique. It seemed as if there was something that they were discussing. I was never given a chance to greet them or even touch them and from the way they were so into their conversation, I could see that they could not see me and if they did then it was never revealed to me. As they discussed, with glorious faces filled with inexplicable joy, I could only imagine if it was possible to be used like these great servants of the Lord.

I looked at them in deep admiration of their ability to work great miracles, see angels and also God' s provision over their lives. Here were men and woman of great renown from Kenneth Hagin who was regarded as the father of faith and his great ability to get limbs to appear from nowhere, to William Marrion Branham who would call animals into existence and had a prophetic unction that you would be a fool not to agree that he had a tremendous gifting in the prophetic.

Whilst I looked I heard the voice of the Lord thunder as he spoke to me.

"How do you want to be used?"

I remember falling down to my knees and then lying prostate on the ground there in heaven. The ground was filled with flowers that seemed to have life. You wouldn't crush them if you could and wouldn't even if you could. They were beautiful beyond words. When I lay prostate on them they simply passed through my body, never crushed, and I felt no pain at all.

I remember answering in a very subdued voice. You see I didn't know how to respond to the voice or how to act. I simply answered from an unrehearsed stance. I did not expect to be asked that.

"I want to prove to the world the existence of God through the power of the Lord to do miracles, signs and wonders that you exist. I want something that separates believers in your son and the religion of the earth. In fact I want what they used to have plus more"

The silence that followed, though in heaven you can't measure time seemed to be an eternity and I did not know whether to repent of just run. I began to think that I had asked the wrong thing. Was I disrespectful to the LORD to ask him about these things?

Why did I ask? All these questions where coming into my mind until I felt the same feeling that came over my body just before the Lord spoke to me about what I wanted, it is that that showed me he was about to speak. However what he spoke was so little but sent chills all over me and exposed the PRAYER BANKS revelation.

"If you want what they have just IMAGINE yourself armed with a LITTLE PRAYER"

With that I was ushered back into my room but my body seemed not to have realised that I was no longer in the heavenly realm. The flesh of my body seemed as if was trying to jump off my bones. I tried to stop it physically but could not. The flesh had experienced the glory but the thought of that question and the answer the Lord gave to me on PRAYER BANKS was very enlightening. All I needed was to be armed with a little prayer.

THE PROBLEM

The biggest problem was that prior to this encounter with the Lord, I had already dedicated a tithe of my time to the Lord with regards to the demonstration of God's power so I prayed at least 2 hours 24 minutes a day, but it seemed the Lord never called it a prayer. He still called that time in prayer an introduction. It was telling that the Lord would tell a man praying to be used in extraordinary levels of power for 2 hours and 24 minutes a day that he needed a little prayer that is longer than what he was doing.

How could he say almost 3 hours was not a little prayer? This was hard but I quickly learnt that what I was doing was nothing so I extended it to 7 hours a day and the miraculous that I can only describe as 'rediculous miracles' began to happen. I figured that I needed a little 7 hour prayer and I made the deposits until my withdrawals were not being accepted by the banking system of heaven.

Let it be known that its not for everyone to do 7 hours in prayer, in as much as 40 day dry fasts are not for everyone, these are supernatural fasts when God gives you supernatural sustanance to bear such fasts. There was a time I did a dry fast for 92 days, it was not for anything specific, but I felt in my spirit I had to do a major deposit in my Prayer Bank, its not something I can tell anyone to do, but you need God to impress something in your spirit before you do such supernatural fasts. The nicest thing about the system of PRAYER BANKS is that they are not congregational in policy, they are individualistic. What works for the other might not be what works for you. However there are a lot of things that work across the board like minimum time of prayer that constitute BANK ACCESS which is 1 hour.

You will see what this revelation will do for you if you dare take it. However you need to learn how to open a bank account before you go deeper with this ancient secret of Prayer Bank Account System.

Opening Your Bank Account

For you to participate and enjoy this wonderful Prayer Banking System you have to open an account. Remember in the Banking system withdrawals and deposits can only be made by account holders. An account gives you power to transact in the Banking system, it gives you a record and a history for your transactions to be monitored. Without an account you will not be able to access the Banking System.

Opening a Bank Account is very simple, you have to receive the Lord Jesus Christ as your Lord and saviour. Jesus Christ is the one who runs the Bank, he is the Bank custodian and the Bank Owner. He is the one who issues accounts in his Banks and all you have to do is get an application form, fill in and submit. No applications are rejected in this Bank, in fact everyone has one reserved for them, it's up to them to come in and get connected in the system. Watch this the bible says;

For God so loved the world that he gave his only begotten Son, that whosoever believeth in him should not perish, but have everlasting life.

John 3;16

Do you notice that Jesus was given for everyone in the world? He is available to each and everyone of us, not to some exclusive club which recruits by invitation only. 'Whosoever' means everybody is invited, do you see the love God has for his creation? He was willing to sacrifice his only Son so that through him he would win the whole world. It's up to the world to know him and receive him so as to start an eternal relationship. Notice;

He was in the world, and the world was made by him, and the world knew him not. He came unto his own, and his own received him not. But as many as received him, to them gave he power to become the sons of God, even to them that believe on his name.

John 1;10-12

God had Jesus, his only begotten Son, whom he sacrificed so that whoever receives Him, would be given power to become a son and daughter of God. This power gives you the right to function and operate like him because with it comes the divine nature of God being imparted into your spirit. His name gives you a power of attorney to access all that belongs to you. That is why you use his name to cast demons, heal the sick and call things into being by using the name of Jesus. That is why Jesus said, if you ask anything in my name i will do it. You see you have been given a power of attorney to act in his stead simply by use of his name.

For you to use his name you have to have a relationship with him, you have to receive him and deepen the mutual relationship with prayer. Any relationship is developed by communication, be it with work mates, in a marriage or even with church folks that's why businesses have retreats so as to cement and deepen teamwork.

The principal holds true with Prayer Banks, you need to open an account first by receiving Jesus Christ as your saviour and establishing an intimate relationship with him through prayer.

You see you can' t use his name at will without a relationship with him, in as much as you can' t make a withdrawal or a deposit in a Bank without establishing a relationship, which you do by opening an account.

By becoming a child of God you have the right to use the name of Jesus. Once a child it is important to grow in the character of Christ by meditating upon his word and growing in prayer. The bible gives a story of certain sons who wanted to make a withdrawal, yet not only did they not have a deposit but they also did not have a bank account. The bible says in the book of Acts;

Then certain of the vagabond Jews, exorcists, took upon them to call over them which had evil spirits the name of the Lord Jesus, saying, We adjure you by Jesus whom Paul preacheth. And there were seven sons of one Sceva, a Jew, and chief of the priests, which did so. And the evil spirit answered and said, Jesus I know, and Paul I know; but who are ye? And the man in whom the evil spirit was leaped on them, and overcame them, and prevailed against them, so that they fled out of that house naked and wounded.

Acts 19;13-16

Three issues arise in this case, the first one is that these folks wanted to make a withdrawal yet there was no record of their deposit. Then they wanted to operate in the banking hall yet they didn' t even have a Bank account and their character was not consistent with the name they wanted to use.

The name of the Lord Jesus is very powerful, Apostle Paul says of this wonderful name;

Wherefore God also hath highly exalted him, and given him a name which is above every name. That at the name of Jesus every knee should bow, of things in heaven, and things in earth, and things under the earth; And every tongue should confess that Jesus Christ is Lord, to the glory of God the Father.

Philippians 2;9-11

These folks had the right name, they used the right name at the right time on the right person. The name of Jesus, is above every other name and every knee, every demon, every sickness should bow at the name of Jesus. So what went wrong with the sons of Sceva? They used the right name but they didn't have an account to use it. Remember our scripture in John 1, you have to be given power to become a son of God and that power is Exousia power, the power that gives you supernatural jurisdiction, it's the power which gives you the power of attorney to act instead of Jesus by use of his name.

In the banking system the account holder can give another person a power of attorney, which gives them the right to act instead of the account holder. They can sign on their behalf and even withdraw on behalf of the account holder on the strength of the power of attorney. Now Jesus gave everyone who has received him Exousia power, to use his name in his stead, that is how you open your bank account, you have to be a son or daughter of God. Your tongue has to confess that Jesus Christ is Lord to the glory of the father.

Withdrawal with No Prayer Bank Account

Now the sons of Sceva had not done that. They didn't have a bank account and there was no relationship. You can't walk into a bank and make a withdrawal or deposit yet you don't have an account, the bank will chase you away unless you open an account. This is what happened to the sons of Sceva, they didn't have an account.

The demons knew Apostle Paul had an account and they knew the name of Jesus. But as for these folks, the demons didn't know them and turned against them. They had written a cheque with the right name but the account was on zero and their names were not on the list of those with the power of attorney!

Withdrawal with No deposits

The second issue is that of wanting to make a withdrawal yet there was no deposit done. Once an account has been opened a deposit has to be made so as to back up future withdrawals. The sons of Sceva wanted to withdraw deliverance yet there had been no prayer made, they didn't have a prayer deposit to back up their withdrawal. So even if they had an account but with no prayer deposit made they couldn't make any withdrawal. You have to make a deposit first before a withdrawal is made. You need to have a prayer deposit made before drawing out the miraculous power of God.

Withdrawal with No Power to use the Account

The third issue raised here is the issue of character of Christ, you see the word 'name' in the text 'the name of Jesus' is the word character, you need the character of Jesus Christ, this is how the power of attorney works. You may have the bank account and have the deposit but for you to access your withdrawal you need your signature on the withdrawal slip and the signature has to match with the signature in the banking system file. You can have money in your account but if your signature or access code doesn't match you will not be able to withdraw what belongs to you.

Character is key, it is important for you to have the character of Christ for you to be able to use his name. These folks didn't have the character of Christ, notice they were vagabonds and they were exorcists they had not received Jesus Christ as their Lord and saviour, they didn't have a relationship with Jesus, to them it was just another fashionable gimmick of exorcism. They wanted to use the name of Jesus yet they didn't have the power of attorney, as they got to the bank the signatures didn't match. That of Paul was there but their signature wasn't there. Though they were sons of the Chief Priest, it didn't suffice, do you see that? It had nothing to do with their relationship with the Chief Priest but it had to be a relationship with Jesus. You have to know Jesus and take up his character for you to be effective and have impact in his kingdom.

Now that you have seen how an account is opened, I want to take a deeper insight into how you can make various transactions including deposits into your prayer bank account before you are able to make withdrawals. This is the essence of maintaining your Prayer Bank Account.

CHAPTER TWO

Prayer Banking Systems

When the Lord spoke to me with regards to this revelation of prayer banks, he told me that there is a banking system in the prayer world that the saints of old used but many believers have not awakened to and that is why many don't pray as often as is required.

In that visitation the Lord reminded me of the scripture that says;

"Pray without ceasing"

He told me it could be taken to also mean;

"Bank without seizing"

That opened my spirit to the need for a deeper prayer life. It was like a neon bulb lit in my spirit, soul and body and all of a suden I could see clearly the power and potency of prayer banking. I began to see the posibilities that those who use this banking system of prayer have and I just wanted, right there and then, to be counted among those who new the Prayer Banking System.

The Prayer Banking institution

To appreciate the banking system of prayer one has to understand that there is a banking institution. This is licensed to accept deposits from the public and has a duty to make those funds available on demand. With the funds deposited, a bank can issue out loans to its clients who are in need of funds. So banks play an intermediary role within an economy, of attracting savings and disbursing then as loans for investment and productivity.

Banking clients open accounts so as to make deposits and build such deposits as savings so that in the event of need they can make a withdrawal for use or transfer funds to whichever beneficiary they choose. You can only make a withdrawal from what you have in an account, if there are no funds in your account you can't make a withdrawal. However a bank can avail a loan facility so that a deposit is made into an account to facilitate a withdrawal but such privileges are forwarded to the bank's clients who have established a reliable track record, whom the bank is sure will be able to make future deposits to expunge the loan or overdraft granted.

Our Prayer Banking Institution

Our prayer life operates much like the banking system, we have to make prayer deposits constantly as a lifestyle to back up any future withdrawals we may want to make in the future. Most Christians miss it because they get so desperate to make a withdrawal from God yet they have never put in anything in prayer. Some only make prayers in emergency situations only to get frustrated and bitter with God when nothing seems to happen.

It is akin to rushing to a bank to make a withdrawal simply because summons have been issued yet you have not made any deposit into your bank account against the summons. You see in such a case you can' t get bitter against your Bank, you will only have yourself to blame.

The bible puts it this way;

Then Peter said, Silver and gold have I none but such as I have give I thee. In the name of Jesus Christ of Nazareth rise up and walk.
Acts 3;6

Look closely at Acts 3;6. It says;

'Such as I have give I thee'

Peter could only give what he had, at that particular moment he may not have had money to give the lame folk, which in no way implies he didn't have money but what he had, which was healing in the name of Jesus, he could give.

You see, you can't give what you don't have, in as much as a bank can't give you a withdrawal where no matching deposit or accumulative deposits have been made, do you catch that? It is a supernatural principal; you can only give what you have, in as much as the heavens can respond commensurate with what you have deposited.

Now let's take a look at how we make deposits into our prayer bank accounts.

Prayer Bank Deposits

A deposit account is a savings account, current account, or other type of bank account, at a banking institution that allows money to be deposited and withdrawn by the account holder. These transactions are recorded on the bank's books, and the resulting balance is recorded as a liability for the bank and represents the amount owed by the bank to the customer. As Christians, our prayers have a record as they come up before God, they do not just evaporate into thin air but God notices, records and remembers them. Let me show you in the word. Watch this;

There was a certain man in Caesarea called Cornelius, a centurion of the band called the Italian band, A devout man, and one that feared God with all his house, which gave much alms to the people, and prayed to God alway. He saw in a vision evidently about the ninth hour of the day an angel of God coming in to him, and saying unto him, Cornelius. And when he looked on him, he was afraid, and said, What is it Lord? And he said unto him, Thy prayers and thine alms are come up for a memorial before God.

Acts 10;1-4

Cornelius was a man devoted to the things of God, he was a giver and prayed to God always. Prayer to him was a lifestyle, it was a way of fellowshipping with God, it was to strengthen a relationship and incidentally he was given to visions. He had an encounter and saw an angel of the Lord, who said his prayers and charity to the poor went up as a "memorial offering" before God.

Clearly, this is the language of acceptable sacrifice. But what is the significance of this particular kind of offering, a "memorial offering"? It means that God thinks of or remembers the person who has done something and for him to remember it means that there should have been an account of sort, where prayers were accounted for and banked and God could access to see how much was being put there.

Notice in the Greek rendering the word 'memorial', means something that enables someone to remember. So if the memorial goes up before God, then it makes possible sense that it functions as a memorial for God to remember something about the one who gives the memorial. Which means for God to remember, it means our prayers are recorded, can actually be monitored and made reference to. For the angel to be sent and make reference to his prayers, someone was noticing, especially given the fact that he had not yet been saved.

Cornelius was an outstanding man and a scripturally significant Gentile. Through him the door of faith to the Gentiles was opened which the bible states in Acts 10:1 - 27. We are told of Cornelius in Acts chapter ten and eleven and how he prayed.

"...prayed to God always"

Acts 10: 2

To him prayer was a lifestyle. He was banking continuously that God chose him to be the first gentile to receive his salvation. This was due to his understanding of prayer banks.

We are also told that God heard Cornelius' prayers even though he was not saved. Cornelius had to hear the gospel and obey it in order to become saved. Notwithstanding, God "heard" Cornelius' prayers before he was saved! Suffice to say, it was his prayer bank account, which made him to be noticed and receive a vision, which led to his salvation through Peter. The angel gave him an instruction to send for Peter who was in Joppa for Cornelius to receive salvation. God saw his heart, being a giver and heard his prayers and it was important to God for him to be saved, to the extent of sending an angel to ensure he receives salvation.

The story of Cornelius reveals not only the basis of prayer bank accounts but it also reveals the importance of the discipline of prayer. Prayer is something, which he did always even though he had not received salvation but for there to be a memorial and a remembrance there has to be a prayer reference point which in our context is your prayer bank account, recording all your prayers as deposits the same way we deposit funds in a savings or current account.

In the first chapter, we indicated that opening a bank account is akin to receiving the Lord Jesus as our savior and here it appears like Cornelius had an account before salvation. It is important to realize that these were the early days of the Christian movement as the gospel and salvation shifted from Jews and opened up to gentiles. In fact Cornelius was amongst some of the very first gentiles to receive salvation and it was his understanding of making prayer deposits, which made him get noticed, and an angel to be sent.

So the emphasis of opening a bank account is tied to salvation, for prayer without salvation is futile, salvation is the most important foundational principle in our Christian walk which is why God sent an angel specifically for Cornelius to be saved. It also shows us that God can hear a prayer of a person who is not saved, but his ultimate will is for people to be saved. That way prayer becomes intimate and has significance.

When you read the scriptures, you not only learn about the content of prayer, but you also notice the discipline and the regularity of it. Both previously, Daniel and the Psalmist prayed three times a day: morning, noon and evening. And this isn't just an Old Testament thing. When you read the book of Acts, the Apostles follow the same basic pattern. It's always told, as incidental to the stories, but regulated prayer is a common backdrop.

Remember the word of God says;

"Now Peter and John were going up to the temple at the hour of prayer, the ninth hour"

Acts 3;1

Then it goes on to say,

"The next day, as they were on their journey and approaching the city, Peter went up on the housetop about the sixth hour to pray"

Acts 10;9

Even the centurion Cornelius, who is described as "an upright and God-fearing man" gets in on the action:

"I was praying in my house at the ninth hour"

Acts 10.1-3, 22, 30

Understand that, the Ancients marked time starting at dawn, which is roughly 6 a.m., making the sixth hour about noon and the ninth about 3 p.m. To this day these two particular hours of prayer are called by their Latin names of 'sext' and 'nonce', following the ancient numbering. Because of these passages and others, such as Psalms 119 in which the Psalmist speaks of praising God seven times daily, including midnight.

The church has from its beginning encouraged "praying the hours." It is important to note that, the point is not about at what time you should pray, no but the point is the discipline of prayer, the fellowship and intimate relationship it establishes and also the regularity of it or how many minutes you spent in the banking hall depositing prayer.

So there's real value in being this disciplined. In fact, it's probably crucial to our sanctification. Disciples of Christ are marked by discipline. We only progress in holiness to the extent we make it a priority.

Many believers spent hours in the banking hall, not depositing prayer but withdrawing or trying to withdraw from an account they never made deposits into. Prayer Banking system sounds exciting but it is a way that promotes more time in prayer than anything. It increases the desire for one to spent time in prayer.

Banking Prayer Is Not Child's Play

That this is hard goes without saying, but that it appears from the scriptures as necessary and beneficial is just as obvious as the sky above you. Even the Lord Jesus knew the importance of pushing hours into his prayer bank and made prayer banking a lifestyle, notice;

And it came to pass in those days, that he went out into a mountain to pray, and continued all night in prayer to God. And when it was day, he called unto him his disciples; and of them he chose twelve, whom he named apostles.

Luke 6;12-13

The point of going into a mountain was simply to seek solitude, to be away from the people and put all focus on being intimate with God. He continued all night praying for his disciples who would take the gospel forward and this was crucial for him as he had to choose the right people, who would take his mission beyond his time on earth. He spent about 12 hours making a prayer deposit because what was before him was crucial; he had to choose twelve apostles from a number of disciples.

The choice of the twelve from the group of disciples was the big withdrawal he had to make but he was aware he could not make such a withdrawal without a big deposit. Such was the life of Jesus. It was that of prayer deposits and commensurate withdrawals. Let's take a look at withdrawals dynamics.

Prayer Bank Withdrawals

When deposits are made into bank accounts, the account holder has every right to make withdrawals against the available balance. Where there are no funds or insufficient funds, appropriate withdrawals will not be able to be made. In such cases an account holder has to replenish their account. It is prudent however that constant deposits are done so as to build a balance so that in the event of a withdrawal there will be a sufficient balance to finance it. Problems arise when emergencies happen and one has to make a withdrawal yet there are insufficient or no funds in the bank account.

The Lord Jesus made prayer banks a lifestyle, it was a process of making constant deposits and in the event of withdrawals he was always ready to sustain them.

JESUS TURNS A MULTITUDE AWAY

Watch this;

And straightaway Jesus constrained his disciples to get into a ship, and to go before him unto the other side, while he sent the multitudes away. And when he had sent the multitudes away, he went up into a mountain apart to pray; and when the evening was come, he was there alone.

Matthew 14;22-23

When you read the scripture in isolation it appears as if Jesus was insensitive to the cause of the multitude to whom he had come to save. This multitude was a spill over from a healing crusade Jesus had held. As if that was not enough he had fed this very multitude of five thousand men, several women and children. This was a massive withdrawal Jesus had made, from healing the sick to turning five loaves of bread and two fishes into food enough to feed the multitude and still remain with leftovers. They couldn' t leave the master but Jesus constrained his disciples to get into the ship and he sent them away.

Now sent away, in no way implies he asked them to leave, he literally sent them away and asked his disciples to leave the multitude. Jesus knew he had just done a massive withdrawal and needed time alone, away from the multitude and even away from the disciples so that he could replenish his prayer bank account in prayer. I understand he had the spirit without measure but also remember the scriptures say he also emptied himself and took on the form of a servant. There ought to be balance you see with all we see in the word.

So withdrawals are the responses of heaven to our account. Withdrawals are the manifestation of God' s dynamic and miraculous power be it for healing, deliverance, the working of miracles, or even praying for business, a tender, a contract, marriage or removal of a mountain along your prophetic path. When Jesus descended from his prayer closet in the mountain he joined his disciples in style except for one thing;

But the ship was now in the midst of the sea, tossed with waves; for the wind was contrary. And in the fourth watch of the night Jesus went unto them, walking on the sea.

> Matthew 14;24

When Jesus came down from the mountain he was so fully loaded, his bank account was so full that he joined his disciples by walking on water. Not only did he walk on water but as Peter joined him on water he pulled him up whilst standing on water. This is how full his account was, you can withdraw for your benefit and for the benefit of others. I will touch on these dynamics when we discuss prayer bank transfers and joint accounts.

As soon as Jesus entered the ship the boisterous wind which jolted Peter ceased. You see when you have a strong bank account you can make withdrawals which defy the laws of nature, you walk on water, stop winds and bail out those who are sinking. As they got to the other side, Gennesaret, Jesus did more withdrawals. Another multitude gathered, which he was prepared for because he had deposited into his account before hand.

Do you see he was a visionary and an extraordinary strategist, he didn't start to pray when he saw the need, he didn't run around to look for a deposit when a withdrawal was on hand, he had already made his deposit and was more than ready to do another massive withdrawal. The bible puts it this way;

And when they were gone over, they came into the land of Gennesaret. And when the men of that place had knowledge of him, they sent out into all that country round about, and brought unto him all that were diseased; And besought him that they might only touch the hem of his garment; and as many as touched were made perfectly whole.

Matthew 14;34-36

Do you see how prepared Jesus was? Before he was sending the multitudes away, but this time the men of the land were bringing the multitudes in, bringing sick folk and when they touched his garment they were made perfectly whole. Jesus had forseen this withdrawal and was prepared for it, it became easy because he had a full account ready to cover such a massive withdrawal. The only question to the healing was if they had touched the garment not whether the power to heal was there. As they touched his garment they withdrew healing anointing and received their healing. You remember the woman of the issue of blood, who also touched the hem of the garment of Jesus yet so many touched him but when she touched him, Jesus said ' i felt virtue, power leaving me' . That was a withdrawal and it sustained a miracle because Jesus was loaded as he constantly replenished his account in prayer. Jesus knew the secrets to prayer banks and also taught his disciples of these hidden secrets.

DISCIPLES MAKE WITHDRAWAL ATTEMPT

Lord have mercy on my son, for he is lunatic, and sore vexed; for ofttimes he falleth into the fire, and oft into the water. And

I brought him to thy disciples, and they could not cure him.
                                                    Matthew 17;15-16

The disciples failed to cast out an unclean spirit of lunacy. This was a withdrawal which they failed to make, yet they had been empowered to make such withdrawals. They had been given power and jurisdiction over unclean spirits and diseases, not just some but all manner of diseases. They had been taught how to cast out such spirits and they had done it before but this time it didn' t work, what could have been the problem because they had jurisdiction over the spirit of lunacy, over the lame, blind, deaf and dumb? Notice;

And when he had called unto him his twelve disciples, he gave them power against unclean spirits, to cast them out, and to heal all manner of sickness and all manner of disease.
                                                    Matthew 10;1

They had been given power before the encounter with the lunatic boy, but they failed to cast out the disease. They had been given a mandate to preach the good news, saying ' the kingdom of heaven is at hand' . They had the unction to ' heal the sick, cleanse the lepers, raise the dead, cast out devils. Freely they had received and freely they were to give, that was their terms of reference, their job description but they failed to cure the lunatic boy.

Jesus didn' t waste time, he rebuked the devil; and he departed out of the lunatic boy and the child was cured. The disciples were astonished, because the way Jesus casted out the devil is the same way they had been taught, they had done as the master had done it but they didn' t achieve the same results.

WHY DID OUR CHEQUE BOUNCE?

The disciples came to Jesus and asked;

'why could not we cast him out?'

The statement shows that what Jesus did, is exactly what they had been taught and done but it didn' t achieve the results. It was tantamount to asking, the Bank Manager,

'why did my cheque bounce?'

You would have written the right amount in figures which match exactly with the amount in figures, the date on the cheque is correct, the signature on the cheque is the same as the signature on the bank' s image file. So what could have gone wrong, why was the cheque denied withdrawal, why did the disciples fail to cast out a small - small demon. Jesus was emphatic;

Howbeit this kind goeth not out but by prayer and fasting.
Matthew 17;21

So the issue was not about the accuracy of the cheque details, their cheque bounced simply because there was insufficient funds in their bank account. They needed prayer and fasting, to make a deposit into their Bank account, so it means they were not praying enough, they were not depositing enough to sustain the imminent withdrawals. Do you see the dynamics of prayer banks, how lack of deposits can compromise your withdrawal capacity. Now lets look at maintaining a prayer bank balance.

Maintaining a Prayer Bank Balance

Another popular Gospel song says, "Just a little talk with Jesus," and perhaps that song better describes the prayer life of most Christians. However, the very minimum every Christian should pray in order to live a victorious life is at least an hour each day. That won't make you an intercessor or a prayer warrior, but it will probably be enough to maintain your present relationship with Jesus. Therefore we can refer to the one hour prayer as maintenance prayer or survival prayer.

Erkenesh Teklemarian, the precious wife of the superintendent in Ethiopia where a revival was rising and many had question on what was required for such a revival to take place in America. She declared to Conference attendees held in Louisiana;

"You must pray one hour just to overcome temptation, but do you believe that revival will come because of this kind of praying? I think not!"

She based this statement on the following verses of Scripture:

"And he cometh unto the disciples, and findeth them asleep, and saith unto Peter, What, could ye not watch with me one hour? Watch and pray, that ye enter not into temptation: the spirit indeed is willing, but the flesh is weak".
Matthew 26:40-41

If you are not regularly praying one hour, make this your first goal, but not your stopping place. At least an hour of prayer every day is required in order to maintain our present relationship with Jesus Christ, to overcome temptation and to help us to live in a way that is acceptable to Jesus. However even this hour is even a minimum in overcoming temptation.

Jesus was a man given to prayer, it was a lifestyle, it was not something he did when he needed something, he did it to maintain fellowship, to be intimate with God, and he taught these secrets to his disciples.

"And it came to pass, that, as he was praying in a certain place, when he ceased, one of his disciples said unto him, Lord, teach us to pray…"
Luke 11:1

Often there is a sad neglect of teaching on how to pray effectively. New converts are told that they should pray, but it is often assumed that they should already know how to pray. We quickly seek to establish our new converts in our Biblical doctrine. We want them to quickly learn the holiness standards of the church, the importance of tithing, and a dozen other subjects that we deem to be very important. But that which will affect their relationship with God the most is sometimes omitted. They have become soldiers in the army of the Lord, but we send them out to fight without any equipment!

It was the prayer life of Jesus that created a hunger in the heart of the disciples to know how to pray effectively–thus their request, "Lord, teach us to pray." Jesus answered them by giving them this prayer pattern:

"After this manner therefore pray ye: Our Father which art in heaven, Hallowed be thy name. Thy kingdom come. Thy will be done in earth, as it is in heaven. Give us this day our daily bread. And forgive us our debts, as we forgive our debtors. And lead us not into temptation, but deliver us from evil: For thine is the kingdom, and the power, and the glory, for ever. Amen."

Matthew 6:9-13

Jesus said, "After this manner pray ye." The pattern He gave was not something that must be repeated day after day in its exact form. Also, it does not include everything that we are to pray concerning. But it does give us the basic pattern for effective praying. Remember that Jesus' prayer example begins with praise and ends with praise in Matthew 6 vs. 9 and 13:

"...Our Father which art in heaven, Hallowed be thy name."

"...For thine is the kingdom, and the power, and the glory, for ever. Amen."

Our prayer time should always begin and end with praise and thanksgiving. In fact, if you are going to pray one hour, thirty minutes can easily be spent in praise and thanksgiving to God. The essence of the prayer was to bring the kingdom, so that the will of God on the earth will be the same as the will of God in heaven.

See, you now have dominion and reign as a king, all your needs are granted because you are now operating in the will of God. It touches on forgiveness and deliverance or rather protection. It is however important to note that this prayer was before Jesus had died and resurrected, because with it came dominion over the devil. However do you notice the prayer had little to do with asking for things, it centers on praise and giving glory to God for his kingdom to manifest in your life.

A life Of Prayer is Key

A life full of Prayer deposits is the key, it is certainly not everything but it answers everything. Jesus never said his house will be a house of miracles, or healing, or prophecy. He said;

My house shall be called a house of prayer

This was because prayer unlocks the domain of heaven and unleashes it's presence here on earth. Make prayer your lifestyle, maintain your bank balance and you will live a victorious life and at times when your deposits are low after you have developed a deeper walk with the Lord you can have access to a facility called overdrafts.

CHAPTER THREE

Prayer Bank Overdrafts

In the banking system ordinarily you can only withdraw what you have deposited in your bank account. If you attempt to withdraw from your account with no or insufficient funds your cheque will bounce back with the withdrawal denied, you will need to run around and get money so that you make the necessary deposit. However in special cases the Bank can grant you a credit facility so that you can access a withdrawal even though you do not have sufficient funds in your account. Such facilities are granted on the understanding that over the course of business a deposit would be made to make the account good. Such facilities may be extended based on a relationship, which has been established over time or by the simple goodness of your bank. That facility is what is called an ' Overdraft' .

Now you need to understand that you can' t just be granted an overdraft facility simply because you are an account holder, the bank will look at your account history and consider your ability to service the overdraft based on your trend of deposits in the account. Where the Bank is not convinced of your trend and capacity, the overdraft facility is denied.

An overdraft facility makes business smooth because transactions are not limited by your credit balance, business life can still go on the understanding that the account will be made good when inflows come into an account.

The same principal applies in your prayer life, based on your intimate prayer relationship with God, prayers will not be answered simply because you have something in your prayer bank account but on the understanding of your prayer relationship. I have always understood that short prayers don' t work but only work for people who do long prayers. There comes a time, though, when you speak things into existence by a simple command. You see, that longer times spent making deposits in your prayer banks can only back up this kind of command.

Notice, prayer is all about an intimate relationship with God. You can' t make emergency prayers when faced by a crisis yet all along there was no bank deposits to talk about. Remember that for you to have a Prayer Bank Overdraft you have to have a prayer relationship, a trend of prayer deposits in your prayer bank account that will enable you to be granted a withdrawal even though your deposits are used up.

Elijah and the Prayer Overdraft

The bible gives us the story of Elijah who used up his withdrawal to the extent of an overdraft such that he had to scurry for cover as he looked for a deposit to make good his account.

Elijah's Bank Account runs out of credit

God instructed Elijah to show himself to Ahab and he would send rain, the very same rain he had stopped earlier for three and a half years by the power of his word. During the drought, Elijah was fed supernaturally by ravens and was also fed by the widow of Zarephath. When God wanted to send rain back, he sent Elijah armed with a word. When Elijah got to Ahab he challenged him by saying;

"...send and gather to me all Israel and Mount Carmel, and the prophets of Baal, four hundred and fifty, and the prophets of the groves four hundred, which eat at Jezebel's table"

1 Kings 18 vs. 19

And Ahab was up for the challenge and gathered the prophets on Mount Carmel.

Elijah made a sacrifice coupled with prayer, he had to sow what he needed most. The bible puts it this way;

And with the stones he built an altar in the name of the Lord; and he made a trench about the altar, as great as would contain two measure of seed. And he put the wood in order, and cut the bullock in pieces, and laid him on the wood and said, Fill four barrels with water, and pour it on the burnt sacrifices, and on the wood.

1 Kings 18;32-33

Notice how Elijah prepared an altar before he prayed, he understood the relationship between a seed and prayer. A seed is a picture of your sacrificial faith, it is an act of faith, it is the sum of your belief. He wanted water and sacrificed what he needed most, it hadn't rained for three and a half years, water was scarce, it was a highly priced commodity but that's what he chose as a sacrifice because that's what he needed most. Notice how he made a trench to contain two measures of seed. That was their unit measure, and he filled four barrels with water and poured over the wood and sacrifices, this was done a second and then finally a third time until the trench which was about the altar was also filled with water.

Prayer Deposit

And it came to pass at the time of the offering of the evening sacrifice, that Elijah the prophet came near, and said, Lord God of Abraham, Isaac, and of Israel, let it be known this day that thou art God in Israel, let it be known this day that thou art God in Israel, and that I am thy servant, and that I have done these things at thy word.

Hear me O Lord, hear me, that this people may know that thou art the Lord God, and that thou hast turned their heart back again.

1 Kings 18;36-38

When his seed was in place, it was time for him to make a deposit into his Prayer Bank Account. And the Lord responded with fire which licked up the water from the trenches, even the stones were consumed by fire. And when people saw it, they fell on their faces and exalted and acknowledged God and Elijah took the Prophets of Baal and slew them by the brook Kishon.

However this was just the beginning of his deposit, he did another deposit for the rain to come. The bible puts it this way;

..The effectual fervent prayer of a righteous man availeth much. Elijah was a man subject to like passions as we are, and he prayed earnestly that it might not rain; and it rained not on the earth by the space of three years and six months. And he prayed again, and the heaven gave rain, and the earth brought forth her fruit.

James 5 ;16-18

Do you realize what James reveals? He is revealing what really backed the words of Elijah, because in the book of First Kings the rains were stopped simply by these words;

"Elijah said unto Ahab, as the Lord God of Israel liveth, before whom I stand, there shall not be dew nor rain these years but according to my word."

1 Kings 17;1

James gives us more insight into the withdrawal of stopping rain, it came after an effectual fervent prayer, it came after a period of deposits had been made. The prayer was made effective because it was heartfelt, it was continued it was a process and a lifestyle of depositing prayers into his prayer bank. When your deposit is fat, big withdrawals appear easy and effortless. He prayed earnestly, he pushed in the spiritual realm until he received a note of victory that a withdrawal is now due to be made.

When it was due time to make another withdrawal of making the rain come, James shows us that he prayed again, therefore you also are like Elijah, if not greater. You also are a human being like him with a nature, feelings, affections and a constitution like him. So even though he was a prophet he still needed to follow the principals of prayer banks. For you to achieve greatness in your prayer life you also need to follow the principals of prayer banks.

Withdrawal

For the rain to come down Elijah sowed water and prayed, the same way he prayed when he wanted to make a withdrawal for rain not to fall. He understood he couldn't take from where he hasn't put in. When he won the challenge with the prophets of Baal he heard the sound of the abundance of rain. Notice the bible says,

...Elijah went up to the top of mount Carmel; and he cast himself down upon the earth, and put his face between his knees.

1 Kings 18;42

Elijah put his face between his knees which is a position of birthing a miracle, he was praying AGAIN that the heaven will release rain. This was his day to make a big withdrawal, after three and a half years of no rain, after a season of praying earnestly, a season of praying effectually he made his withdrawal. He knew such a big withdrawal wouldn't happen without a big prayer deposit. Even though he had received the word of the Lord that he had to go and show himself to Ahab and God would send rain he had to sow a seed and make a prayer deposit before he could make a big withdrawal.

An Abundance of Rain

Elijah's withdrawal came as a sound of abundance of rainfall, it was a sound but there was no rain nor were there any clouds, just the sound was enough for him to act upon it. He sent his servant to go and look out towards the sea but there was nothing, there was no sign of rain nor was there a sign of a cloud. This didn't move Elijah, he kept sending his servant seven times and on the seventh time, he came back with a good report that there was a little cloud, like a man's hand. Notice Elijah didn't give up, he wasn't moved because he couldn't see the rain in the physical, he knew the deposits he had done, he knew the word he had been given and he held on because his deposit was sufficient to carry his withdrawal.

...And it came to pass in the mean while, that the heaven was black with clouds and wind, and there was a great rain. And Ahab rode, and went to Jezreel. And the hand of the Lord was on Elijah; and he girded up his loins, and ran before Ahab to the entrance of Jezreel.

1 Kings 18;45-46

From a sound of abundance, to a small cloud, the heavens were black with clouds and they emptied themselves with great rain. The heavens released a withdrawal based upon the prayer deposits that had been done by Elijah.

However something interesting happened after Elijah had made his big withdrawal.

Elijah runs into Overdraft

Elijah had won the challenge he extended to the Prophets of Baal, he had made them a public spectacle, he was just one against four hundred and fifty prophets of Baal, but it's never about the numbers against you, it's about the hugeness of your deposits in the bank account!

The prophets of Baal called upon the name of their gods, from morning to noon but there was neither voice nor any that answered. They even cut themselves until blood gushed out but all their efforts were futile. Elijah called upon the Lord God who answereth by fire and he consumed everything on the altar. Over and above that he slaughtered all the Prophets of Baal and then made a big withdrawal by calling for an abundance of rain. All these exploits, these withdrawals were backed by the word of God and the prayer deposits he had made. Now watch this;

And Ahab told Jezebel all that Elijah had done, and withal how he had slain all the prophets with the sword. Then Jezebel sent a messenger unto Elijah, saying, So let the gods do to me, and more also, if I make not thy life as the life of one of them by tomorrow about this time. And when he saw that, he arose, and went for his life, and came to Beersheba, which belongeth to Judah, and left his servant there.

1 Kings 19;1-3

Literally Elijah ran away from Jezebel yet he had just single-handedly slaughtered hundreds of prophets with a sword. He ran for dear life when Jezebel sent a messenger with a 24-hour death threat. The very same prophet who called fire from heaven, who called for an abundance of rain after three and a half years took flight!

He fled from Jezebel yet he had just slaughtered hundreds of the Prophets of Baal. What had happened, what had changed, why would Elijah run away?

Prayer Banks

It is because his prayer bank account was now empty, he was running for dear life, he couldn't make any withdrawals and there was not enough time to make a deposit to withstand the death threats. He had to run around and do something about his bank account status for it was in the red. He had exhausted all his credit. He was on minus balance and the only thing was for him to get an overdraft facility.

But he himself went a day's journey into the wilderness, and came and sat down under a juniper tree; and he requested for himself that he might die; and said, It is enough; now, O Lord, take away my life; for I am not better than my fathers.

And as he lay and slept under a juniper tree, behold, then an angel touched him, and said unto him Arise and eat. And he looked, and behold, there was a cake baken on the coals, and a cruse of water at his head. And he did eat and drink, and laid him down again. And the angel of the Lord came again the second time, and touched him, and said, Arise and eat; because the journey is too great for thee.

And he arose, and did eat and drink, and went in the strength of that meat forty days and forty nights unto Horeb the mount of God.

1 Kings 19;4-8

Elijah was distraught, his prayer account was empty, he couldn't make a withdrawal, he was running into an overdraft and desperately needed to make a deposit. He ran into the wilderness, a place of solace for him to be with God, for him to commune and fill his account once again. He was on the verge of giving up, he wanted God to take his life but his mission was not complete. His prayer for death was not even granted, instead an angel touched him the first time so as to eat and he did eat and drink but laid down. The second time the angel came and woke him up to eat again because the journey was too great. Then he arose and the food was sufficient to sustain him for 40 days and 40 nights. What the angel did was tantamount to granting him an overdraft facility, it was special supernatural food to give him strength for a special journey of fasting and prayer, do you see that?

Remember overdrafts are granted when you have exhausted your credit so as to operate from a deficit on the understanding that you will make deposits in the future.

What he got was supernatural food to give him strength for a special fasting and prayer session for him to make special deposits back into his account. Notice the four hundred and fifty prophets of Baal were fed from the tables of Jezebel, now he had to launch a divine onslaught on the principality of the prophets of Baal, Elijah had to bind the 'strongman', Jezebel and needed a forty day and night fasting and prayer to make a commensurate deposit so as to withdraw against Jezebel.

When his Prayer Bank Account was made good the word of the Lord came;

And the word of the Lord came to Elijah the Tishbite, saying, Arise go down to meet Ahab King of Israel, which is in Samaria...

And of Jezebel also spake the Lord, saying. The dogs shall eat Jezebel by the wall of Jazreel.

1 Kings 21;18 & 23

Notice, earlier Elijah fled from Jezebel and went to beef up his prayer bank in solitude, praying and fasting over a period of 40 days and 40 nights, his account was overdrawn and had to go and make good his account before he could make a withdrawal. When his account had been regularized he came back with the full backing of his prayer bank account and did a withdrawal which was done from a position of strength. He was no longer on the run, he didn't fear Jezebel anymore instead he came in full force and gave a prophetic decree against Ahab who repented and against Jezebel who remained adamant and unmoved by the prophetic word.

Eventually the word came to pass and the book of 2 Kings 9 records how Jezebel was thrown over the window at the instruction of Jehu. She was thrown and some of her blood was sprinkled on the wall, and on the horses. When they wanted to bury her they found no more of her than her skull, her feet and palms of hands, which was consistent with the word of the Lord, which he spoke by his servant Elijah the Tishbite saying ' In the portion of Jezreel shall dogs eat the flesh of Jezebel.

The withdrawal Elijah made came to pass, but only after he had made significant and commensurate deposits into his account, though he had to run as his account was running into overdraft. He knew the secrets of prayer banks, he knew the importance of solitude and seeking the face of God as he deposited into his prayer bank account.

It's important to realize that with overdrafts there are limits and in special cases an account holder can be granted a withdrawal when there is no money in the account or even when the overdraft limit has been stretched beyond. This is solely based on the relationship of the account holder and bank taking cognizance of the value of the client. The story of Moses is also illustrative in this instance.

MOSES' PRAYER BANK

Moses employed a Prayer Overdraft. I want you to see here in the book of Numbers after Dathan and Korah had disrespected him and got people to be against him.

Now Korah, the son of Izhar, the son of Kohath, the son of Levi, and Dathan and Abiram, the sons of Eliab, and On, the son of Peleth, sons of Reuben, took men; And they rose up before Moses, with certain of the children of Israel, two hundred and fifty princes of the assembly, famous in the congregation, men of renown. And they gathered themselves together against Moses and against Aaron, and said unto them, Ye take too much upon you, seeing all the congregation are holy, every one of them, and the Lord is among them; wherefore then lift ye up yourselves above the congregation of the Lord?

Numbers 16 vs 1-3

When Moses heard this, he fell facedown. Then he said to Korah and all his followers,

"...Even tomorrow the LORD will shew who are His, and who is holy; and will cause him to come near unto him..."

Numbers 16 vs. 5

Moses could have dealt with these dissidents in the camp but didn't bother to do it that day. His power could not be displayed that day. You see I have always wondered why he didn't do it that day until the Lord taught me on prayer banks.

Moses knew there was need for him to declare what he was going to do but there was a greater need to go and deposit prayer in the bank vaults of heaven so he could display the power he had promised Dathan and Korah. Moses knew he needed an overdraft and he exposed it by faith and went full force that he promised a display the following day and God made his promise come to pass for everyone to see. God himself allowed him to work with the prayer overdraft then made it come to pass the following day after he had loaded. Watch this;

And it came to pass, as he had made an end of speaking all these words, that the ground clave asunder that was under them; and the earth opened her mouth, and swallowed them up, and their houses, and all the men that appertained unto Korah, and all their goods. They, and all that appertained to them, went down alive into the pit, and the earth closed up on them; and they persihed from among the congregation. And all Israel that were round about them fled at the cry of them; for they said, Lest the earth swallow us up also. And there came out a fire from the LORD, and consumed the two hundred and fifty men that offered incense.

Numbers 16 vs. 31-35

So he withdrew first before depositing in his bank account of prayer. So prayer became the surety to secure the promise Moses had made to Dathan and Korah. God opened the ground based upon the prayers Moses had made after the challenge given to Dathan and Korah.

You can declare something in your life, but if you fail to back it with prayer, that thing you speak is as good as saying "twinkle twinkle little star, how I wonder what you are" and expect a miracle.

God allows his people to declare things even if their prayer bank account is very low, then gives them power to withstand time of prayer so they see the results of the prayer they would have made before the day.

YOU CAN DO IT

It is high time you understand that God calls you;

"The apple of his eye"

In other words, God allows you to hear him and talk to him but above all, he allows you to deposit something after you have used it. He allows overdrafts. He accepts that there are times when you are running on zero in your prayer bank where you can simply speak things into existence even before you back your statements in prayer.

A lot of Men of God have used this trick, with much success, for as long as you go back after the declaration and back it up with prayer. It is akin to writing and issuing a cheque, knowing that it takes a few days to clear, whilst its still going through the mill you run around to look for a deposit to cover the withdrawal. In special cases one can make a request and be granted an overdraft to cover cheques or withdrawals issued like in the case of Samson.

Samson granted an Overdraft

The birth of Samson came with a divine visitation of an Angel of the Lord to a woman who was barren. The angel delivered good news that though she was barren she would conceive and bear a son. With the news also came an instruction that no razor would come on his head and there was a divine mandate upon his life, through him God would deliver Israel out of the hand of the Philistines. The woman bore a son, and the child grew and the spirit of the Lord was with him. Samson would later kill a lion with his bare hands but that was just the beginning as he would later kill thirty philistines and with a jawbone he killed a thousand men.

As his strength and might was displayed, the philistines sought to kill him by recruiting Delilah to entice him so as to reveal the source of his strength. Delilah was persistent until she broke the secret code after three attempts. Delilah pressed him daily with her words and urged him, so that his soul was vexed unto death. Samson relented and revealed his prophetic secret, that his strength was embedded in his hair, being a Nazarite from the womb. That is the moment the enemy struck, shaved his hair and captured him. They even plucked out his eyes, but his hair began to grow.

It was only after his eyes were plucked out that he gained focus of his mission, because his eyes had moved from the ball and got distracted by women. As he regained focus his hair began to grow at a prime venue as many philistines had gathered to celebrate his demise. Samson, who was not a prayerful person. There is no record in the whole bible that he even made one prayer request in his life before this, he did not draw from any prayer bank account but drew out from an overdrawn position. Watch this;

And Samson called unto the Lord, and said, O Lord God, remember me, I pray thee, and strengthen me, I pray thee, only this once, O God, that I may be at once avenged of the Philistines for my two eyes.

Judges 16;28

Samson made a withdrawal, by calling upon the Lord and pleaded for remembrance, he requested strength,

'only this once'

That statement denotes a special request, which acknowledges that he was desperate and didn't have anything to back him up. For him, his request was to avenge his two eyes, which still bore testimony of his lost focus, but really the request was in line with fulfilling his divine mandate of beginning to deliver Israel out of the hand of the Philistines.

His overdraft facility was granted and he took hold of the middle pillars, which supported the roof of the building, and the building fell upon the people therein and the philistines who died with him were more than all whom were killed in his lifetime.

Operating from on Overdraft Position

Operating from an overdraft position is certainly not the perfect will of God, remember the bible says;

'Owe no man nothing except love'

The ideal position is to have a lifestyle of prayer where an optimal bank balance is maintained and as and when need arises withdrawals are made. You can' t treat God as an errand boy where when you are in a tight spot you make emergency short prayers, as alluded to, short prayers are for those who have made long prayers, in as much as special withdrawals are for those who have been making deposits.

Overdrafts ordinarily are granted to those who have an existing relationship, who are known to make regular deposits, whom the bank is aware that even if they grant the special overdraft facility it will be made good eventually. So overdrafts indeed come in handy in emergencies but invariably they are granted to those who have made prayer a lifestyle except in special cases like Samson.

Overdraft In Manchester

I remember one day in Manchester at a hotel we were renting as a church where I had need to use my overdraft. You see I had been conducting a prophetic service for over 5 hours or so and I could feel the power go out of me to heal and do other things. People were receiving direct and accurate words of Prophecy as usual and many were being healed but as the Lord said once;

"I felt power go out of me"

I also felt power going out of me that I had to just wrap up the service. However, before I did the manager of the hotel stormed in to the service with such indignation and lack of respect for what the Lord Jesus stood for. I was so filled with righteous wrath but I could not demonstrate anything supernatural towards him because the anointing had lifted or let me say my bank account was used up for me to respond supernaturally. I needed to load up my account.

The only power left was for me to use in finishing the service. Now those who really don' t understand the dynamics of the anointing will take this assertion to be unbelievable because they use only faith to minister yet the prophetic relies on the prophetic grace to be in operation. You see I can prophesy with blinding accuracy, calling your name, address, describe your house and all the intricate and intimate details you can think of. All this I can do all the time and anytime of the day but for what I say prophetically to be effective in a person' s life I have to be sensitive to the anointing.

So the hotel manager stormed into the room with me standing behind the podium. He came right at me and just blurted out that he was now locking the door so he needed us out. I reasoned with him that I was left with just ten minutes to finish service but he would not have it. He started hurling all sorts of insults at the Lord and how useless what we were doing was and that' s where you wont go with me if you want us to even talk.

I remember throwing him out of the room and him calling the security guards in order to get us out even before our agreed time was up. It is in that moment with everyone looking that I asked the Lord for something beyond my prayer bank balance. Some of the church members had been disturbed by the man hurling insults at the Lord and really were physically available to do harm if necessary and I knew that was going to really be contrary to what the scriptures would have us do so I prayed for something beyond my prayer bank balance and the Lord came through for us.

He gave us an overdraft. He spoke to me to mark a line on the carpet for this atheistic group, three of them to be exact. Then he told me to tell them;

"Whosoever thinks that the Lord Jesus is useless and does not exist and wants to test his power should cross this line now"

They looked at each other with such sarcasm that it irritated me but the Lord was at ease as usual. No rushing whatsoever. He spoke again to me to speak to them and I opened my mouth to give them the word of the Lord.

"We are not going to harm you with our fists. The lord simply is going to prove to you that he exists and wants to save you. He loves you"

With that I felt power well up in me and these men were still laughing at me. I could feel the small congregation we had then since it was Spirit Embassy's formative years were also fearful that nothing was going to happen but as they stood there the unimaginable happened. The first guy walked towards the line in order to cross it and fell just an inch behind it and so did the second and the third in that order. They started trembling under the power of God and their faces full of confusion. We just took our people back into the service and did thirty more minutes describing the power of God. We had a nice time in the Lord and a great time using my overdraft facility that the Lord had extended to me before those former atheists.

When we closed service two of them were still trembling under the power with one of them sitting down and one of our protocol guys explaining to him what had happened.

God had come through for us and extended an overdraft facility when my bank balance was on the low and he can do the same for you if you have a relationship with him as the bank. Remember you need to understand that you can't just be granted an overdraft facility simply because you are an account holder, the bank will look at your account history and consider your ability to service the overdraft based on your trend of deposits in the account. Where the bank is not convinced of your trend and capacity, the overdraft facility is denied.

However, overdrafts are for getting by, but there are times when you need another person to join their money with yours so that you pull your resources together for a big purchase. This is called a Prayer Bank Joint Account.

CHAPTER FOUR

Prayer Bank Joint Accounts

A Joint account is a bank account shared by two or more individuals. Any individual who is a member of the joint account can withdraw from the account and deposit into it. Usually, joint accounts are shared between close relatives, spouses or business partners. The joint account holders have to agree on the terms of their account, and one of the most important terms is the signing arrangement when making withdrawals. Should all signatories appear, it should be known which signature is key. These are ordinarily called main signatures and which signatures are minor. The account holders have to agree on the parameters for the account to operate smoothly.

There are circumstances where you may want to make a deposit into your prayer bank account jointly with others but there has to be an agreement over a matter which binds you together. The bible puts it this way;

Again I say unto you, That if two of you shall agree on earth as touching any thing that they shall ask, it shall be done for them of my Father which is in heaven. For where two or three are gathered together in my name, there am I in the midst of them.

Matthew 18;19-20

Do you see the principles are similar to a Bank Joint account? There must be at least two people, who must agree on a specific matter. The choice of the partner is really up to you, but what is important is you have to be in agreement with this particular partner, as in the matter must bind you together. You can' t choose someone who is far removed from the issue on hand.

For example, if you want a tender as a business, it will be prudent to have a prayer bank joint account with a partner who is in the same business with you and who is also looking to God for that particular tender to come out favorably. Whilst you can be in agreement with an independent person, the choice of someone who is dependable and who has a stake in the matter is paramount. For the tender you can' t simply walk out of the gate and ask a stranger and say ' I want a tender, can you join me for a prayer of agreement?'

You see an agreement is paramount, the amplified version says;

"...if two of you on earth (harmonize together, make a symphony together)..."

Matthew 18;19 (AMP)

It gives you the picture of an orchestra which can have tens of musical instruments, each with its tune but when they play together its in harmony such that together it makes a symphony, in other words the instruments play much better together than as individual instruments. There is a multiplier effect, the sum total is greater than individual simple effect because of synergy. The reason being, you are in agreement and there is harmony and you have gathered in the name of Jesus, he also is in the midst to give symphony to the harmony and give the multiplier effect.

What binds the agreement is the name of Jesus, the spirit and the minds of the partners should be in one accord and more importantly their speech should be one. You can't achieve anything if your joint partner has doubt over the matter or his faith levels are questionable.

Let's look at the tower of Babel for a moment;

And the Lord said, Behold the people is one, and they have all one language, and this they begin to do, and now nothing will be restrained from them, which they have imagined to do. Go to, let us go down, and there confound their language, that they may not understand one another's speech.
Genesis 11;6-7

Do you see the power of agreeing on a matter, they agreed to the extent that God did not see them as a people for he said;

"the people is one"

He saw them in one accord as one unit, and when peoples' spirits and minds are in agreement absolutely nothing can be retrained from them whatever they have imagined it will be granted. The only way God could have stopped this phenomenon was to break the agreement and he executed that by confusing their one language. They failed to understand each other and they parted ways.

Now watch the opposite of what happened in Genesis here in the book of Acts;

And when the day of Pentecost was fully come, they were all with one accord in one place. And suddenly there came a sound from heaven as of a rushing mighty wind, and it filled all the house where they were sitting. And there appeared unto them cloven tongues like as of fire, and it sat upon each of them. And they were all filled with the Holy Ghost, and began to speak with other tongues, as the spirit gave them utterance.

Acts 2;1-4

Notice, they were in one accord, which means they were in one spirit and one mind, they were in agreement and in one place and above all they were gathered in the name of Jesus and Jesus kept his word;

"...there am I in the midst of them".

Matthew 18;20

He sent the Holy Ghost which filled all of them and they began to speak one language of heaven, tongues. From this in filling, the gospel spread and is spreading all over the world. It was this one accord, power of agreement, which broke the chains of Paul and Silas.

Prayer Joint Account

As the Apostles were spreading the gospel to the uttermost ends of the world, they knew the secrets of prayer banks. It was their lifestyle to pray and make regular deposits into their accounts because of the vagaries of the territory which didn't want the gospel to spread. Not only did they make prayer their lifestyle, they knew the advantage of prayer joint accounts;

And it came to pass, as we went to prayer, a certain damsel possessed with a spirit of divination met us, which brought her master's much gain by soothsaying…

But Paul, being grieved, turned and said to the spirit, I command thee in the name of Jesus Christ to come out of her. And he came out the same hour.

And when her masters saw that the hope of their gains was gone, they caught Paul and Silas, and drew them into the marketplace unto the rulers.

Acts 16; 16-19

The disciples carried their one accord into their prayer life. They knew they had to maintain their prayer bank accounts, they knew they had to constantly make deposits but above all they knew the power of corporate prayer, the multiplier effect of prayer joint accounts.

Notice, the bible says;

"as we went to prayer",

It didn' t say,

"as we made our prayers"

No it doesn' t say that. It says they went into prayer. It says as 'we', as one, in one accord and in agreement. This was something they would do as a lifestyle not because there was an emergency. It so happened that as they were on their way to lavishly furnish their prayer joint accounts they met a soothsayer and notice, it was Paul who made the withdrawal and cast out the spirit.

Notice, Apostle Paul said very few words, it was a simple but powerful command because it had the backing of deposits which had been made. The spirit left within the hour, but this caused a furor as the spirit was a money maker. The masters apprehended Paul and Silas and they were brought before magistrates, the multitude rose against them and they were beaten and cast into prison. Though they were beaten up, and in chains, they couldn't imprison their prayer joint bank accounts. The Bible says:

Who, having received such a charge, thrust them into the inner prison, and made their feet in the stocks.

And at midnight Paul and Silas prayed, and sang praises unto God; and the prisoners heard them.

Acts 16;24-25

Though they had been chucked into inner prison, not just prison but inner prison. Inner prison is for high risk seasoned criminals with records of jail breaks. They were also in stocks, which are leg irons; this couldn't rob their joy nor could it rob their prayer bank accounts.

Paul and Silas, were in the same place and in the same predicament, but being prayer partners their spirits and minds were one, they were in one accord, agreeing on this matter at hand. There had been wrong application of the law and blatant victimization as the magistrates were biased because of the ruckus caused by the multitude.

The Joy of a Prayer Bank Joint Account

It takes people with joy within to sing praises to God, it takes people with the backing of strong prayer bank accounts to pray and sing so loud that other prisoners will hear you. It was the audacity of faith, that in times of trouble, they were found singing praises. They were not complaining, they were not bitter against God, nor were they divided, because its in times of trouble that you see how strong partnerships or agreements are. Such circumstances would have been ripe for the two to have differences perpetuated by accusations and counter accusations.

After all it was Paul who cast out the spirit, in the strict sense it was Paul who got grieved and caused all this, but because they were in one accord, they didn't take it that way they stood in agreement on the matter of justice, they prayed for divine extra judicial and territorial power to intervene on earth and heaven responded.

And suddenly there was a great earthquake, so that the foundations of the prison were shaken; and immediately all the doors were opened, and everyone's bands were loosed.

Acts 16:26

Do you see the power of a Prayer Joint Bank Account? Do you see the power of agreement, the power of having one accord and speaking the same language? Notice the multiplier effect, it was Paul and Silas who prayed from the inner prison but an earthquake shook the foundations not of the inner prison but of the entire prison, it was not just the doors of Silas and Paul's prison cell which was let loose. The bible says 'all the doors were opened' and notice 'everyone's bands were loosed', everyone, not just of Paul or Silas but everybody's bands were broken because of the multiplier effect of the power of prayer joint bank accounts. Do you see how powerful prayer joint accounts are? I have used Prayer Joint Accounts with success.

Using My Wife's Account

When our second child was born with one kidney in Ashton-Under-lyne' s Tameside Hosiptal on the 8th of May 2007 we had a real problem on our hands. I was hearing God and I had preached on healing so many times that my teachings were coming back to haunt me not because I doubted God on healing but many preachers who had heard my predicament where now having a field day.

I stood on God' s prayer Bank revelation but nothing seemed to work until one day I chose to get my wife' s prayer bank account on my side and we made a joint account for weeks praying for the recreation of the second kidney. It took some time but when we joined our accounts it seemed suddenly the burden lifted and to the shock of the doctors our son developed the other missing kidney.

Our joint account was working!

Now prayer joint accounts govern people in agreement on a matter but I want you to learn another thing that is very exciting which the Lord taught me called a bank guarantee which gives a bank account holder the right to accrue a liability on the understanding that if the Bank account holder fails to settle the liability, the bank will cover it.

CHAPTER FIVE

PRAYER BANK GUARANTEES

A Bank guarantee gives a bank account holder the right to accrue a liability on the understanding that if the Bank account holder fails to settle the liability, the bank will cover it. Essentially a bank guarantee enables the bank account holder to acquire goods, buy equipment, or draw down on the guarantee thereby expanding activity beyond bank account holder. It effectually gives you surety to transact and trade on account with the counterparty extending goods to you based on the credit risk of the bank and not the credit risk profile of the account holder.

For example, Joe Bloke wants to secure a 300kva generator to power a farming project from Perkins for 50 000usd, he doesn't have enough funds in his account to purchase the generator for cash but can pay it in installments over time. Perkins only sells generators for cash but for AAA clients it can give generators on account. Any other clients who do not have an AAA credit rating it would not ordinarily deal with them but for anyone else with a lower credit rating it will only sell on account if there is a Bank guarantee. A bank guarantee means if Joe Bloke defaults the Bank will pay, so it is as good as Perkins has extended the generator to Joe Bloke's bank. So it is the name of the Bank, it is the credit rating of the bank and not of Joe Bloke that grants the generator to Joe Bloke. So when Joe Bloke is armed with a Bank guarantee, it is as if the bank has gone on a buying spree.

Only For Clients With A Track Record

Bank guarantees are extended not to just any person who walks into the Bank. They are extended to clients who have a relationship and a track record with the bank. Bank guarantees are extended to clients who are known, who have a history and have a reputation with the bank.

Put differently, Banks are only willing to issue bank guarantees to clients who have the same character as the bank. The character of a bank is based on trust. It's based on being reliable that if you leave money with the bank and you come at whatever time you will be able to withdraw your money. By the same token, the Bank will issue a bank guarantee to someone who it trusts will be able to pay back in the event it has to call for payment. For the bank to be convinced, it has to monitor the account history of the client and see if it has the same character as the bank, which pays upon demand.

A bank does not want to soil its name because all the bank has is its name. Once it loses its reputation its name is soiled and this will compromise its ability to do business. The biggest asset of the bank is its name and that is the strength of a Bank guarantee, the name of the bank will make its clients go places.

YOUR GUARANTEE

As Christians our life is that of faith, and that faith is based upon the word of God. Faith is our currency as believers and that is how we access our rights and privileges in Christ. Without faith it is impossible to please God and by faith God has given us a name that is above every name, which we can use. On our own we are able to effect limited change in this world but there comes a time when we need to access a guarantee from a higher authority. We access a higher authority by using the name of Jesus in a decree or declaration. In fact in all banking system this name is compulsory. You need it to bank no matter who you are. Now watch this;

And in that day ye shall ask me nothing. Verily, verily, I say unto you, Whatsoever ye shall ask the Father in my name, he will give it you. Hitherto have ye asked nothing in my name; ask, and ye shall receive, that your joy may be full... At that day ye shall ask in my name, and I do not say to you that I shall pray the Father for you; for the Father himself loves you, because you have loved Me, and have believed that I came forth from God.
John 16;23-27

Jesus was talking to his disciples and revealing to them secrets of prayer. You see, he was saying ' on that day you shall ask me nothing' , in reference to the day he will be glorified after resurrection when he will be with the father. From that day, they would ask the Father directly because before, in the old covenant, access to the Father would only be through the priest. Now, direct access was granted because Jesus became our great High priest to access the Father. He was very clear that his name was a guarantee that whatsoever you shall ask of the father in his name;

'he will give it you'.

You see you don' t need any go between to get to the Father, you don' t need any mediums because the name of Jesus gives you direct access. A medium would ' pray the Father for you' but you see he is not a medium by using his name it' s as if Jesus is asking for it. It' s akin to the Bank guarantee where it is no longer the name of a third party which counts but it is the name of the bank that counts.

This guarantee gives you trust that whatever you will ask the Father you will be granted, and it is this trust which builds your faith. You have a guarantee that because you have used the name of Jesus, it is settled the same way one who is armed with a Bank Guarantee would have the confidence to purchase whatsoever he desires with the guarantee that the Bank will back him up.

Onoma

However as alluded to earlier in the first chapter, when we discussed the 'character', that the word 'name', is the word 'onoma', which means character, in other words, for the name of Jesus to be fully functional you need to take up the character of Jesus. In the same vein, a Bank will give a Bank guarantee to an account holder who has the same character with the Bank. It is the character of a Bank to be credible and pay on demand and as such a bank will give a guarantee to a client who has a track record of doing business with the bank. In essence, the name of Jesus will function when you have the character of Christ, and Christ had a character punctuated with prayer and fellowship with the Father.

GOD KIND OF FAITH

When you have the character of Jesus, you will function like God, you will have faith like him, you will love like him, you will be holy like him, you will forgive like him, you will carry his glory and it will be evident in your life. There are realms of faith and the epitome of faith is the God kind of faith. In your prayer life there is a special kind of prayer called the prayer of faith, which draws out from your faith levels, the deposit is really your level of faith, for there is no faith, weak faith, little faith, great faith and the God kind of faith. You see faith is likened to a mustard seed because it is like a seed, it is something that comes in a small way, simply by hearing the word of God, but your response to what you hear will determine what level of faith you will get to.

Faith is like a muscle, it needs to be exercised until it reaches its epic levels. So the word of God, is your guarantee, it is your back up like a merchant who is out to buy equipment armed with a bank guarantee, his buying power is essentially determined by his level of faith. Now watch this;

And Jesus answering saith unto them, Have faith in God. For verily I say unto you, that whosoever shall say unto this mountain, Be thou removed, and be thou cast into the sea, and shall not doubt in his heart, but shall believe that those things which he saith shall come to pass, he shall have whatsoever he saith. Therefore I say unto you, What things soever ye desire, when ye pray, believe that ye receive them, and ye shall have them.

Mark 11;22-24

Jesus was just not talking about any kind of faith here, for him to say ' have faith in God' it means your faith can be placed on a Doctor, on your self or in some other individual, but he said much more than ' have faith in God'. In the Greek rendering, essentially he was saying;

'have the God kind of faith'

In other words, operate with the faith levels God operates in. You see, God has faith, he uses faith, in fact the world came about because of faith. When he said, ' light be' he had faith that light will be drawn out and appear from darkness, the bible puts it this way;

Through faith we understand that the worlds were framed by the word of God, so that things which are seen were not made of things which do appear.
Hebrews 11;3

It was through faith that this world was made, God had faith in his word that what he speaks will appear, he believed that by his words what we now see, the moment he calls them forth, they would materialize. This is the kind of faith Jesus is talking about in Mark 11;22-24, those are the faith levels you should operate in, for you now have the character of Jesus.

Notice how the word;

'...saith...'

Or

'...say...'

This is emphasized in contrast to the word ' believe' . He says whoever shall ' say' to this mountain, but shall ' believe' what he ' says' he shall have what he ' says' . Three times you should say, what you believe and notice, he didn' t say, ' say what you have' he said ' you shall have what you say' . God didn' t have the earth, but he believed he would have it and he said it, he called it into being, he didn't say what he had, for there was darkness. Most folks say what they have, they say their situation instead of saying what they believe for them to have what they say.

Do you catch the difference, when you have been diagnosed of a high blood pressure, folks say, ' I have a high blood pressure' or ' my blood pressure is high' , they are saying what they have not what they believe. When you need healing you say what you believe for you to have what you say. So you declare,

'I thank God for my healing, in the name of Jesus'

If that' s what you believe and say it, then Jesus say' s you shall have what you say. In the context of the scripture, the mountain to be removed is the sickness. If one believes in their heart and not doubt that it will be removed and believe that it will come to pass, then what you have declared you will have it. This is the essence of prayer bank guarantees, it gives you the audacity of faith to decree and declare things into being by faith that you have full backing of the name of Jesus drawing down from your faith.

Notice one essence of the prayer guarantee of faith from the scripture we discussed above;

'Therefore I say unto you, What things soever ye desire, when ye pray, believe that ye receive them, and ye shall have them.'
Mark 11;24

When you do a prayer of faith, because it is something that should be done once and that settles the matter it is important to note when you actually receive what you desire. Notice, it says 'when ye pray' not after prayer but when you pray, 'believe that ye receive them', it doesn't say when you see the results with your eyes, it says when you pray, that's the moment you believe you have received 'and ye shall have them' in the physical. You don't believe when you see, you believe you have received when you pray 'and ye shall have them', that's why a prayer of faith can be done once, it's a declaration, it's the audacity of faith. The very same way one who has been issued a bank guarantee, he already believes the generator is settled once the bank guarantee is on hand not when the generator is delivered. That is why faith is an evidence, it is a substance and is the title deeds of what we hope for and not perceive with our physical eyes. Notice;

Thou shalt also decree a thing, and it shall be established unto thee; and light shall shine upon thy ways. When men are cast down, then thou shalt say, there is a lifting up...

Job 22; 28-29

Prophesy Into Your Own Life

A Prayer Bank guarantee gives you the audacity to declare things into being, it gives you the unction to prophesy into your own life. It gives you your authority and position as a King to declare things and have them established. Notice when people are cast down, you will not say what you see with your physical eyes but what you believe in your heart, you will say (decree and declare) what you have been guaranteed and what you draw from your faith. The bible says, then you will say ' there is a lifting up' and you shall have what you say. You see a Bank guarantee gives you a different kind of language, you begin to talk your future truth and move into it, because you now walk in the light of the revelation that ' you will have what you say' not ' say what you have or what you see' . Notice the bedrock of your guarantee;

And this is the confidence that we have in him, that, if we ask anything according to his will, he heareth us; And if we know that he hear us, whatsoever we ask, we know that we have the petitions that we desired of him.
1 John 5; 14- 15

A Bank Guarantee gives you confidence to walk to any merchant and buy whatever goods, because you know that since the Bank has issued it and has signed the guarantee, they can' t renege on their word. That alone gives you confidence and buying power that whatever you purchase, it is guaranteed by the Bank and you already have it. Our scripture talks of ' according to his will' , now that doesn' t mean whether God likes it or not, remember he has already given the guarantee, the issue is his word is his will, have you done it according to his word. In as much as a Bank will give you a guarantee according to their ' word' , according to their prescribed criteria. And his will is to declare in the name of

Jesus Christ, you see, its as if it is Jesus who has done it, you are using his name in as much as a Bank guarantee doesn' t use the name of the Bank account holder but the name of the Bank to secure goods.

Do you see that? Do you see the ancient secrets of Prayer Bank Guarantees embedded in the word of God? Do you see how much authority you have by the power of the tongue, do you see how you can prophesy, by speaking forth into your life. The only thing that determines your buying power or extent of withdrawal by Prayer Bank Guarantee is your faith level and your character, in the context of ' onoma' , the character of Jesus Christ we discussed earlier. Go out and grow your faith, building up yourself upon your most holy faith and light shall shine upon all your ways.

Now that you understand prayer bank guarantee, we need now to look at Prayer Bank Transfers, where your deposit can be transferred for the benefit of another in need.

CHAPTER SIX

Prayer Bank Transfers

In the course of Banking business, the main transactions are deposits and withdrawals but within the banks and banking system, banks transfer funds from one account to the other within the same bank or even to another bank. For this to be approved, sufficient funds need to have been deposited in the account. Ordinarily withdrawals are for the benefit of the account holder but Bank transfers are done under instruction of account holder for the benefit of another account holder.

Stephen died because the church was not in prayer so it could not make a transfer to save him and yet Peter survived because the church's account was full of prayer deposits and they managed to do a transfer for his benefit.

Why Stephen Died

The bible talks of Stephen, who was full of faith and power, and did great wonders and miracles among the people. He was on fire for God, he had zeal for the things of God such that when he spoke they were not able to resist the wisdom and the spirit by which he spoke. Unfortunately his words were misconstrued and turned against him and were presented before the council as blasphemy against Moses and against God.

Stephen's distracters also stirred up the people as false witness to build up their case of blasphemy. He was given a chance to speak his side of the story, which he did with much passion but this didn't exonerate him, instead it cut the council to the heart and they apprehended and cast him out of the city and stoned him to death. This was done in the full presence of Apostle Paul, whom at that time was a persecutor and instigator of violence against Christians. However, eventually he converted and became a notable Apostle. They stoned him to death, as Saul (Apostle Paul) watched but he was not the only one who did nothing to abort this injustice.

The church was still in its infancy and fear had gripped them, as there was great persecution against the church to the extent that they scattered and were not in one accord. Notice;

And Saul was consenting unto his death. And at that time there was a great persecution against the church which was at Jerusalem; and they were all scattered abroad throughout the regions of Judaea and Samaria, except the apostles. And devout men carried Stephen to his burial, and made great lamentation over him. As for Saul, he made havock of the

church, entering into every house, and haling men and women committed them to prison. Therefore they that were scattered abroad went everywhere preaching the word.

Acts 8;1-4

Do you see how the devil unleashed his plan, he wanted the gospel to be destroyed, not to reach the uttermost ends of the world, by killing the apostles and persecuting the church. This was done by instilling fear and breaking their one accord, but they didn' t manage to break the apostles, they remained resolute and in one accord and in a way the persecution worked in their favour because that way the word was preached abroad. Do you see how God can turn persecution or anything to your good.

When Prayer Banks were used for Peter

When the wind of persecution struck again this time it was aimed straight at Apostle Peter and not the young and new preachers like Stephen, you see we are not ignorant of the devil' s devices. He shifted focus from the new members to the head, so that the movement would be leaderless and visionless. Watch this;

Now about that time Herod the King stretched forth his hands to vex certain of the church. And he killed James the brother of John with the sword. And because he saw it pleased the Jews, he proceeded further to take Peter also.

Acts 12;1-3

They had killed Stephen by stoning, James was next by the edge of the sword and next in line was Peter, who was the head. This was the final blow, the final nail in the coffin to the movement of the gospel for where there is no shepherd the sheep will scatter.

Previously the church had been reduced to mere spectators, griped by fear but when they apprehended Peter a Prayer Bank Transfer was made. Notice;

And he saw that there was no man, and wondered that there was no intercessor...
Isaiah 59;16

An intercessor is a person who is aware of his priestly responsibility of praying for others. Through intercession God bestows on us the opportunity to make great impact in the lives of others. Through intercession you can sway the edge and the stones of the enemy, but there has to be someone who stands up to become an intercessor.

Notice our scripture from Isaiah, ' he saw that there was no man and wondered that there was no intercessor' , do you see why Stephen and James died, no one stood up to intercede, to pray for their situation as if it was their own because everyone was running around in fear. Now the edge of the sword was being prepared for Peter and that is when intercessors stood up, that is when they made deposits into their prayer banks and made a withdrawal, a transfer for Peter. Watch this;

And when he had apprehended him, he put him in prison, and delivered him to four quarternions of soldiers to keep him; intending after Easter to bring him forth to the people. Peter therefore was kept in prison; but prayer was made without ceasing of the church unto God for him. And when Herod would have brought him forth, the same night Peter was sleeping between two soldiers, bound with two chains: and the keepers before the door kept prison.

Acts 12; 4-6

Interesting timing from Herod, at a time the church will be celebrating Easter, which marks the resurrection of Jesus, that is when he wanted to kill Peter. That would have been a symbolic execution for it would have shaken the centre at a time the church would have been celebrating the resurrection and life of Jesus Christ. The church may have sat back and watched the death of Stephen and James without an intercessor being found, but this time they stood up and made a corporate prayer bank deposit and transferred it to Peter's account who apparently was sleeping.

This was not just an ordinary deposit, the bible says;

"but prayer was made without ceasing of the church unto God for him"

Using this revelation you can say;

"...but Prayer Bank Transfer was made without stopping to the bank account of Peter"

Prayer Banks

Something they didn' t do for Stephen or James, do you see that?

So a deposit was being done, in fact it was a corporate joint deposit being done but not for their benefit but the deposit was being transferred into Peter' s account for a grand withdrawal.

Now watch what took place after the transfer went out of the church account of Prayer to that of Peter;

And, behold, the angel of the Lord came upon him, and a light shined in the prison; and he smote Peter on the side, and raised him up, saying, Arise up quickly. And his chains fell off from his hands. And the angel said unto him, Gird thyself, and bind on thy sandals. And so he did. And he saith unto him, Cast thy garment about thee, and follow me. And he went out, and followed him; and wist not that it was true which was done by the angel; but thought he saw a vision. When they were past the first and the second ward, they came unto the iron gate that leadeth unto the city; which opened to them of his own accord, and they went out and passed on through one street, and forthwith the angel departed from him.

Acts 12;7-10

The Prayer Bank Withdrawal was a classical jailbreak to say the least, the church made a prayer deposit continuously and made a transfer to Peter who was asleep and had to be woken up by an angel. This move was after the church had already lost Steven and James and it was high time they did something to avoid Peter being killed. Even for Peter it was too good to be true, he thought he was in a vision when he saw the angel leading him and gates opening before him. It was not too good to be true for Peter only because when he came to the house of Mary where the church was gathered praying, still making prayer bank deposits, they were shocked to see him and thought they were seeing his angel.

The church kept depositing not knowing the transfer withdrawal had already been made by Peter. Do you see the power of prayer bank transfers, do you see the power of intercession, how much power it has and what changes it can make. They were now into deeper areas because they kept on loading his account even after the Prayer bank transfer had been accepted by God.

When I used a Prayer Bank Transfer

I started having visitation from the Lord and from Angels at the age of five but there came a time when I was seventeen that the lord told me at the age of twenty seven there would an explosion of visitation and true to his word it happened and still takes place.

However my wife still was very low on visitations and had not seen the Lord in a visitation but only heard him audibly and saw angels many a times so I would tell her what the Lord would have said when he visited me but that got to a time that it wasn' t sitting well with me anymore.

Prayer Banks

At that time we had one child, Uebert junior and he also at the age of close to five years old was also experiencing visitation so my wife was now the only one left. That was until one day I asked to be locked into a room for a whole week so I could pray. In the midst of the prayer depositing week I got into a visitation from the Lord and I boldly asked for my wife to also have a visitation and suddenly the walls that separated the prayer room and our bedroom where she liked to spend time in prayer, disappeared and I could see her from the prayer rom and she could also literally see me.

I told her to take a pen and paper and then it happened. She began to se the Lord as clear as I was seeing him and he began to speak to us both and our notes were identical after the visitation. I had just transferred prayer credits to her account, which was low with regards to visitations of the Lord. I had just experienced prayer bank transfers.

You see I have made a lot of prayer bank transfers to some men and women of God through impartation and that has changed their stories. God has the ability to make you create a bank transfer.

Transfers Are Important

Prayer bank transfers are important but for a big order to be delivered and the overdraft and all the joint accounts are exhausted there are times where you need to see the Bank Manager.

CHAPTER SEVEN

When You Have To See The Bank Manager

In the normal course of banking, one can operate an account by simply going into the banking hall to do deposits, withdrawals and transfers without the need of seeing the bank manager. In these days of high end technology, you can actually effect transactions without even stepping into the banking hall, as you can do your banking transactions via the internet or even your cell phone. However there are instances when you need to see the bank manager, this is not an everyday thing, but there are special cases where you have to seek audience with the bank manager.

In the banking system, managers attend to special requests like loans, review of overdraft limits, and issuance of bank guarantees, letters of credit to facilitate imports and exports, advisory services among other specialized services. However it is important to realize that such opportunities and services are usually extended to people who have a relationship with a bank, people with a history and track record of doing proper business with the bank. The same applies for your prayer bank system, there are special instances when you have to see the bank manager or owner so as to present your case for it to be entertained.

BANK OPEN DOOR POLICY

The door of the bank manager is always open for account holders, especially those who maintain their accounts well and by virtue of being an account holder you have every right to have access into the bank manager's office so as to present your case before him. Depending on the merit of your case, it is up to the bank manager to grant you your requests.

Notice;

Come now, and let us reason together, saith the **LORD**; though your sins be as scarlet, they shall be as white as snow; though they be red like crimson, they shall be as wool. If ye be willing and obedient, ye shall eat the good of the land; But if you refuse and rebel, ye shall be devoured with the sword; for the mouth of the **LORD** hath spoken it.

Isaiah 1;18-20

Do you see that the door is open for you to come in and reason with the Lord. In our context the Lord God is our bank manager and owner who is giving you an invite to come in and present your case. Now notice, it's open to everyone, even if your sins are as red as scarlet that is not what He looks at. The issue is on how strong you reason and argue your case before him. A lot of Christians are not aware of this right and privilege that they can reason and argue with God in prayer. Look, he is a father, the same way my kids argue and reason with me and based upon their merits I can grant and turn down their requests. I do that with my children because I love them and have a relationship with them, also because they know who they are and what belongs to them, they know in special cases I can go and talk to Dad, present my case, reason with him and get what I want. When I reason with them, I do not look at what they may have messed up before, that's past and forgiven, I can't hold that against them. I simply look at the issue at hand and based on its merits I can grant it or turn it down.

The reason why Christian folks don't do this is twofold, they are not aware they have this right and also because they have a sin consciousness. To them they always feel inadequate before God, to reason and argue with him because of their sins, which have been forgiven, forgotten and washed away. That is why Isaiah says, even though your sins are as scarlet, which is a deep red color, they shall be washed away, in fact they have already been washed away and they shall be as white as snow. So when you present yourself, it is no longer you being seen but God begins to see his son Jesus before him. That is why the bible puts it this way;

For we have not an high priest which cannot be touched with the feeling of our infirmities; but was in all points tempted like as we are, yet without sin. Let us therefore come boldly unto the throne of grace, which we may obtain mercy, and find grace to help in time of need.

Hebrews 4 vs 15-16

Jesus is our merciful and faithful great High Priest who stands to make reconciliation for the sins of the people, yet he was without sin because he became sin and by his blood washed the sins away, bearing all curses, transgressions and our infirmities.

So when you get a hold of this, you will remove your sin consciousness and take up a Christ consciousness, which gives you an identity of who you are and gives you a deeper knowledge of what belongs to you. With this consciousness you will be able to come boldly upon the throne so as to obtain mercy and find grace in time of need.

So essentially you visit the bank manager in time of need, but notice you are not alone, you have a High Priest, who stands like your advocate or lawyer as you present your case. When a judge has a case before him, he deals with your lawyer as opposed to you directly; when he has seen your lawyer he has seen you. The issue then is your ' willingness and obedience' to the principals or requirements of the bank manager as you present your case before him. Where there is success, Isaiah says you will eat the good of the land, you will have success and will have prosperity but where you refuse and rebel, which could be out of a sin consciousness or mere ignorance of who you are, you will be destroyed by the sword.

Now your invitation is not an opportunity to miss, abscond or waste, it's your opportunity to present to argue, contend, and reason with strong arguments so that you can get approval of a special case before you. Look this prayer banking system is for special cases, it's when you have to have a miracle at all costs. Notice;

Produce your cause, saith the Lord; bring forth your strong reasons, saith the King of Jacob.

Isaiah 41;21

AND;

Put me in remembrance; let us plead together, declare thou, that thou mayest be justified.

Isaiah 43;26

DEPOSIT

When you have a special case before you, you can't afford to pray amiss, your deposit then becomes your strong reasons, your declarations, your pleas as presented in your supplication or petition which effectively is your withdrawal. Your strong reasons are your argument against a situation on hand. This is usually like an impossible situation, a desperate situation where you need a miracle at all cost. Whilst previously your prayer deposit was simply based on your prayers, in this case you also need a deposit of the word inside you. You will need to present your arguments backed with the word of God, then present it back to God.

It's the same case with a bank. Let's say you have a special request of a loan, the bank will give you their word, in other words their requirements, to the extent that if you satisfy these requirements, you will be granted a loan which you desperately need. Over and above that, the bank will ask you for security against the loan and once you satisfy their requirements, there will be no reason the bank can deny you a loan.

The security you have in this situation is the word of God, so essentially you are putting God in remembrance of his very own word, you are pleading backed by his word, you are reasoning with him standing on his word and you are declaring standing on his word. That is your security, which you present and deposit before the bank manager. Now it means if you have no word inside you, if you have not meditated upon the word, it means your arguments will be weak and your pleas or requests will be turned down.

This book of law shall not depart out of thy mouth; but thou shalt meditate therein; day and night, that thou mayest observe to do according to all that is written therein; for then thou shalt make thy way prosperous, and then thou shalt have good success.

Joshua 1;8

You deposit the word inside your spirit by meditating upon it day and night, by reading it and depositing it inside your spirit, when it has filled your heart, there is no way it will depart from your mouth because out of the abundance of the heart the mouth speaks. When the word is inside you and you do as it says it will make you prosperous and give you good success. Do you see how you eat the good of the land?

When you don' t have the word inside you, you can' t present a strong case before God, you can' t present strong reasons which will make your case justified.

You see when you present the bank its requirements, backed fully with security the bank has no choice but to grant you a loan. Their application form is like a law unto themselves, that is exactly how the word of God is to him, it' s a law and he has placed it above his name. It is like a parliament which makes laws and statutes. Once the bills are gazzetted into law, even the parliamentarians who crafted the laws have to live by those very laws. They are not above the law, they have to comply in line with the laws, together with everyone else who was not part of the crafting and drafting of the law. Notice;

...for thou hast magnified thy word above all thy name...
Psalms 138;2

Do you see that God has magnified his word above his name? He has placed his word above himself, he can' t go against his word, it is a law unto himself and once you put him in remembrance of his word he has now wriggle room out of it. So when you place him in remembrance it is essentially his word. Which is why it is paramount that you know the word and have it in your spirit so that you can have something to withdraw from, as you present it to him. Remember you can only withdraw from what you have in your account.

In this case you are before the bank manager making requests and arguments to be granted a loan into your account so that you can make a withdrawal. It is for impossible and desperate situations where you need a miracle at all cost. It is for cases where the situation on the ground is very contrary to what the word of God says about you. It is in cases where the devil is throwing darts, despising you, throwing sickness, throwing storms and winds placing an injunction in your movement.

LOAN FACILITY APPLICATION

A bank manager would ordinarily give you a loan application form so that you present your cause before him. Banks are there not only to take your deposits and facilitate withdrawals, but they are there for you in your time of help and need. All you need is to come boldly before the Bank Manager, present your case, backed by strong reasons and arguments. If you are willing and obedient to the requirements its guaranteed your application can't be turned down because an application form is a law unto the bank, they can only invite you to get one when they are prepared and when they have the capacity to grant you.

A loan application has to be written, it's not like a transfer which you can simply do online without even entering the banking hall. It has to be put down and presented to the bank, showing cause why you need it. Why you need the Bank to help you in a desperate situation. Do you know how it works?

The principal is the same with this type of prayer bank deposit and withdrawal, it's a special kind of prayer for desperate situations, when you need a miracle at all costs, it is the only type of prayer which you need to sit down and write.

I exhort therefore, that, FIRST OF ALL, SUPPLICATIONS, prayers, intercessions and giving of thanks, be made for all men;...
1 Timothy 2;1

A lot of Christians are ignorant of the secrets of prayer banks, beyond that they do not know that God wants them to reason and contend with him the way any good father would talk with his children. There is also something Christians are ignorant of; there is an order to prayer banks. Notice our scripture, it says first of all, supplications, which is a prayer for the impossible. You see prayer is not a haphazard affair, God is a God of order. Notice also that the words are in plural which means they can be prayed over and over again until you receive a note of victory in your spirit. Supplications are for a special order, when your situation is desperate and you need a miracle at all cost.

See I have heard people saying 'your miracle is around the corner' yet they never show us the corner, to such I have always had a problem. If my miracle is around the corner, then please show me the corner and I will go to the corner myself and collect my miracle. The prayer of Supplication is the corner. Now the word supplication is a legal word, in as much as a loan application is a legal document. Supplication means a petition, it is a formal request addressed to an official person, or to an organized body, having power to grant it.

It essentially can be broken down into;

An approach; which is made by applicant, just like how you would come into the office of a Bank Manager.

Presentation of Request; done by the supplicant, to a body which has the capacity to grant request. In our context this is a loan application form.

Response; by the body which entertains the request. This is the response of your application by the bank.

In Roman Law, supplications were used as a way of appeal against a verdict or judgement or as a means of rectifying inadequate legislation. In our context we are going to use supplication as an application for a loan from the Bank, in times of desperate need when we need a miracle at all cost.

The word supplication is from the Greek word deesis, which means an entreaty, a petition or request. It is a formal written application carrying evidence requesting a formal body for a specific action. In our case we are looking for a special deposit in our prayer bank for us to make a withdrawal, bearing in mind that a withdrawal can only be made when there is credit in our account. The only way we can have credit in our account is if we make a deposit, receive a transfer from someone or the bank grants us a loan facility into our account. So our deesis, our supplication and our loan application is a well written document requesting audience from the Bank Manager, presenting strong arguments which we reason and contend before we are granted the loan facility.

So our success is dependent on the strength of our cause, it depends on the merits of our case, it depends on the security of our application. Notice;

The LORD has heard my supplications; The LORD will receive my prayer.

Psalms 6;9

Do you see, the power of supplications, it strengthens the order exhorted by Apostle Paul, that first of all Supplications before any prayers, that's why our scripture says, you have heard my supplications, the Lord will receive my prayers. It also implies that your supplications may not be heard, because it depends on the merits which have been presented, it depends on the strength of the arguments and the extent you have gone to place God in remembrance of his word.

WITHDRAWAL

The bible gives us a withdrawal made by Hezekiah when he was sick, the situation was desperate, he was on his death bed, it was an impossible situation, he needed a miracle at all cost. His funeral arrangements were already being planned, hush - hush talks were already being whispered in the corridors of power on who was going to take over. The bible puts it this way;

In those days was Hezekiah sick unto death. And Isaiah the prophet the son of Amoz came unto him, and said unto him, Thus saith the LORD, Set thine house in order, for thou shalt die, and not live.

Then Hezekiah turned his face towards the wall, and prayed unto the LORD And said, Remember now O LORD, I beseech thee, how I have walked before thee in truth and with a perfect heart, and have done that which is good in thy sight. And Hezekiah wept sore.

Then came the word of the Lord to Isaiah, saying, Go, and say to Hezekiah, Thus saith the LORD, the God of David thy father, I have heard thy prayer, I have seen thy tears; behold, I will add unto thy days fifteen years. And I will deliver thee and this city out of the hand of the king of Assyria: and I will defend this city.

Isaiah 38; 1-6

When You Have To See The Bank Manager

Hezekiah was not just sick, but was sick unto death and his death was certain because Isaiah the prophet confirmed it and at least he had been extended time to set his house in order. God had spoken and his Prophet had confirmed it. The Prophet did his job, to deliver the news, whether good or bad news, it is the duty of a prophet to speak what God has spoken. Upon hearing the news, Hezekiah was presented with an impossible situation, he needed a miracle at all cost.

He had the revelation of prayer banks, specifically the prayer of supplication, he knew that the door was open to see the Bank Manager, he knew there was an invite open to present his case before the Bank Manager backed by strong reasons and arguments. He didn't complain or cry, instead he turned his face towards the wall, which represents going in a place of solace, a private place to seek the face of God, it's akin to going to see privately the bank manager for a private talk.

The first thing he did when he prayed was to place God in remembrance, he said 'Remember now O Lord', he was placing his application on paper, bringing his strong reasons showing cause why death was not his portion. He placed God in remembrance of how he walked in truth, which is his word, in other words he was a doer of the word. He was reminding God of his word, he was presenting his security before the bank manager; he was placing the rules of engagement back to the one who set the rules. He reminded God of his perfect heart, which inclined towards his word and reminded him of his works, which were right in his sight, and his sight is determined by his word.

Notice, Hezekiah had no means of extending his life, God had spoken, it was beyond Doctor's and Pharmacists. He did not have enough credit in his prayer bank to command his sickness away, he needed help from the Bank itself, his account couldn't help him, no bank transfers could and no joint accounts would suffice. Only when he sought an appointment with the bank manager did he manage to get recourse. That is when he presented a loan application and was granted and his account was lavishly furnished.

God spoke again through his servant Isaiah the prophet, that he had heard his supplication, he had seen his loan application, he had received his deesis, his petition which was backed by strong reasons and arguments and his application had been a success. Hezekiah was not only given healing but was also given an extra fifteen years, deliverance and defence. That was a big withdrawal, which needed a special order, it needed a loan application to back it up for it was an extraordinary miracle for God to change his mind. As a sign that he had changed his mind, the hand of time was reversed by ten degrees, the earth reversed its orbit around the sun and time was gained to signify additional time being given to Hezekiah. Surely if God could reverse astronomy he could reverse the sickness of Hezekiah.

The Will of God Concerning You

Pray without ceasing. In every thing give thanks: for this is the will of God in Christ Jesus concerning you.

1 Thess 5;17-18

Do you see the secrets of prayer banks? Do you see how you can move the sun and change your world by what is in your prayer bank account? God wants you to live a victorious life of joy, peace, health, wisdom and prosperity but all this is embedded in your prayer bank account, his will is that you pray without ceasing, making deposits into your account, this way no weapon can come near you for you will be more than ready to make a withdrawal against it. Prayer should be your lifestyle, pray for others, intercede for them, make your supplications, have a relationship with the Father, fellowship with him and meditate upon his word, this way your life will move from glory to glory.

Lightning Source UK Ltd.
Milton Keynes UK
UKOW05f1032300114

225556UK00001B/1/P